PUG PASSION

PUG PASSION

An Everyday Guide for Pug People

SAMUEL ADAMS

Published by ROC Publishing 2016

DISCLAIMER

The information contained herein has been posted in good faith and is to be used for educational purposes only.

The author has made considerable efforts to present accurate and reliable information in this book. However, the author does not take any legal responsibility for the accuracy, completeness, or usefulness of the information herein. The information in this book is not intended to provide specific advice about individual medical or legal questions. This book should not be considered a substitute for a reader's own independent research and evaluation.

This book may contain links or refer to other web sites, and other web sites may refer to this book. Links to web sites outside of this site do not imply endorsement or approval of those sites or the information they contain. The links to other web sites are provided solely as a convenience to users of this site. The author is not responsible for the accuracy of the information, the content, or the policies of such sites, and shall not be liable for any damages or injury arising from the content or use of those sites.

This content may refer to organizations, businesses, and other resources available through government, nonprofit, and commercial entities. Referrals to such entities are provided solely for informational and educational purposes and as a convenience to the user. A referral to a product or service on this web site should not be considered an endorsement or recommendation of that product or service. The author shall not be liable for any damages or injury arising from the use of or connection with such products, services, or entities.

TABLE OF CONTENTS

All dogs are unique individuals, they learn and act according to their own exclusive set of circumstances.

This book covers breed standard norms for Pugs, in all their **gorgous goofy glory**.

Forward

Ready to be seduced by those gregarious, fun-loving, clownish Pugs? With their stubborn natures and utter devotion to their humans, this charming breed is very popular and can fit in with most lifestyles.

This book offers a complete and comprehensive look into the life of a Pug from their mysterious beginnings in ancient China to where one may acquire their own Pug.

Covering every stage of a Pug's life from birth to the golden years; this informative book also discusses medical issues, nutritional needs, fun activities and training tips.

Delving into some of the quirkier habits of the breed and stories from Pug enthusiasts, this easy to read guide is for anyone who's interested in knowing more about the breed, Pug enthusiasts who may relate with the stories and everyone in between.

Chapter 1:
Send in the Clowns

"Multum in parvo" a Latin term meaning a lot in a little package. "Multum in parvo" is the Pug motto, it describes the breed beautifully. A 15 pound dog with a 1000 watt personality.

No one is sure where this phrase came from, or how it came to be associated with these wonderfully gregarious creatures, but if the saying fits, use it.

A pack of Pugs is called a "Grumble".

Quite often dog enthusiasts refer to certain breeds as regal, dignified, or even elegant. While some Pugs have an air of dignified grace about them, more often than not, they can be regarded as the lovable class clown.

Charming, playful, docile and stubborn; these are a few adjectives to describe the Pug breed. Any Pug parent will describe (in detail) the length their dog will go to get a reaction.

Because Pugs are, first and foremost, people pleasers. They love their families and will do anything to grab and retain their human's attention.

Due to their compact size, Pugs are perfect for either an apartment or house. Because of their blasé, I love everybody attitude, they are also highly recommended for novice dog owners.

Pugs are very dependent on their humans; this will be a recurring theme throughout the book. They don't tolerate being left alone for long periods of time.

What is this "Stranger Danger"?

Pugs are incredible family dogs. Tolerant of everyone and everything that comes through the door of a busy household, they like to be the center of attention and often will give their families quite a show. **Anything for a laugh.**

Pugs love their people; this can't be stressed enough. With their borderline human obsession, they won't be prone to wandering aimlessly away from the house.

Their mid-level energy doesn't require a five mile jog every morning. Pugs are most happy with a jaunt around the block couple times a day, as long as there is a warm lap to curl up in when they come home.

Curiosity and the Pug

Pugs are an inquisitive bunch, which can land them in some hot water if not properly supervised. A vigilant approach to dog rearing maybe in order for the new Pug parent. Better to keep these canine sleuths safe.

Independent yet lovable

Occasionally they may be regarded as a bit willful; there is potential for some Pugs to exert their independence by taking a stance against training. This doesn't mean they are slow or dimwitted, on the contrary, Pugs are smart. They also have a stubborn streak. If there isn't proper motivation to learn, the dog won't see the point in training.

Gender Neutrality

When choosing a Pug, whether puppy or adult rescue, the question remains, male or female? Is there a difference?

Actually, yes.

While most people chalk it up to preference, there are a few minor differences between male and female Pugs. Research has shown male Pugs have a tendency towards willful snarkiness during their teen phase. The teen years fall some time between 1 and 3 years of age. They often mellow after maturity sets in. That being said, it is often the female that is referred to as more independent than the male. It has been shown that females are a tad easier to train. Females tend to live slightly longer, 13.2 years, compared to males who, on average, live 12.8 years.

A multi-faceted breed

One of the talents Pugs are known for (in the Pug community, anyway) is their ability to fall asleep anywhere. Not only that, but they've also been known to snore their way through anything. Pugs do snore. They also drool quite a bit. It's part of their enduring charm.

Because of their go with the flow approach to life, Pugs are excellent clothing models for those parents that frown on the naked Pug body. To keep their model-like Puggish curves, owners need to monitor their dog's food intake. Pugs tend to put on weight easily, due to their love of food and lower energy levels.

My pug Shadow is aptly named; he follows me EVERYWHERE, including the bathroom. Last winter I was down with the flu. Shadow ran when I did to the bathroom. He stayed by the door as I retched into the commode. When I was finished, I walked slowly out of the bathroom, Shadow looked distressed. I asked him if he was okay and he promptly vomited on my bare feet. Pug empathy, there's **nothing else like it!**

Chapter 2:
A Royal History

This ancient and spiritual breed may be traced back to the time of Confucius. Back then Pugs were called Lo-sze and were the companion of choice for Buddhist Monks in Tibet. Soon the Lo-sze were revered by Chinese nobility. Once European trading began, the Lo-sze caught the eye of Holland's Prince of Orange, who began calling the breed Mopshond.

Speculation surrounds the Pugs origins. Some believe that they are descendants of a type of short haired Pekingese.

Others feel the Pug is some sort of a Bulldog cross or may be a diminutive edition of the Dogue de Bordeaux (French Mastiff).

No one is 100% sure where these Velcro dogs came from, but they can all agree that they are living up to their original reason for being bred; as companion dogs.

British invasion

The Pug made its way into the hearts of the English sometime in the sixteenth century. It's here when the name was attached.

The nickname "Pug" was associated with a monkey or a dog. Some people used the term because the dogs flat face looked like a monkey.

It was the Reverend Pearce that wrote the word "pug" is from a Latin word "pugnus" which roughly translates into human fist. The dog's face may resemble the shadow of a clenched fist.

There is another theory believing Pug is a derivative of Puck, a character from one of Shakespeare's "A Midsummer Nights Dream".

Noble roots

Royalty plays a huge part in the breeds continued existence. In the Chinese imperial household, female pugs were given the same rank as Emperor Ling To's wives. All Pugs living in the palace were under the protection of the royal guard. Anyone attempting to steal one of these beloved dogs would automatically be sentenced to death.

Marie Antoinette, Queen of France, owned a Pug while a teenager in Austria. Her little companion was lovingly named Mops. Then again, maybe not so loving. All Pugs were called Mopshounds, Mops for short, throughout Europe. C'est la vie.

Messengers of hope

Surprising as it may seem, Pugs served their country during the war, in the 17th century that is. They were used as trackers to find people and as guard dogs. Their warning barks would signal when someone approached.

Josephine Bonaparte adored her Pug named Fortune. So much so that she turned her nose up at her marriage bed until Fortune was welcome into the bed as well. Josephine also used her beloved companion to deliver notes to her husband while incarcerated. The notes were concealed under the dog's collar.

Dogs of inspiration

During the Victorian era in England, the Queen developed a special interest in the Pug and began breeding them. She shared her residence with many of these dogs. Because of her association with Pugs, the Kennel Club was started in 1873.

The Duke and Duchess of Windsor (More commonly known as Edward VIII and Wallis Simpson) continued the royal admiration as they resided with dozens of Pugs. When the Duke passed away in 1972, his devoted Pug, James, reportedly mourned his late owner; so much so that it is said that James died of a broken heart.

A royal breed indeed, the Pug have been adored by holy men, royalty, modern day celebrities and everyday common folks. A breed for everyone.

A fold by any other name

Legend suggests the Ancient Chinese have a thing for skin folds. They were always looking for folds or wrinkles in people's faces that look like characters in the Chinese language. That is probably why the Pug is so incredibly loved in Ancient China. Is there another face with more folds and wrinkles than a Pugs?

Modern love

It isn't royalty and holy people who are Pug enthusiasts, there are several modern day celebrities that take their precious Pugs with them everywhere.

Rob Zombie, filmmaker and lead singer for the heavy metal band White Zombie is often accompanied by his black Pug, Dracula.

Scottish actor, Gerard Butler, shows his softer side when he tools around town with his fawn Pug, Lola on his lap.

Tori Spelling, reality star, has a special place in her heart for her late Pug, Mimi LaRue.

Freemasonry

They have their own order, the Order of the Pug. When the Catholic Church banned Freemasonry, this order chose the Pug for their symbol. The members felt the Pug represented what they were, loyal and trustworthy

Chapter 3:
Acquiring a Pug

Pug Fever, it's sweeping the world and everybody wants one. But what is the best way to acquire one? That depends on the individual. There are generally three routes to go. Find a breeder, adopt from a rescue/shelter or for the truly ambitious, become a breeder. In this chapter we'll cover all three alternatives and list the pros and cons of each option.

Keep in mind
Pugs are wildly popular. So much so that they have been bred, over bred, and interbred over the past several decades.

OPTION ONE- FIND A BREEDER

For those potential Pug parents that want to start from the beginning, they may purchase their bundle of joy from a breeder. Ask friends and family members if they know of any Pug breeders. The American Kennel Club (AKC) lists respectable breeders on their site. Pug Forum sites also have lists of "suitable" breeders.

Investigate

Once the list of breeders has been narrowed, it's time to go and check out the facilities where these puppies are being reared.

Things to keep a lookout for are

- Cleanliness- are the dogs and areas clean?

This should be self-explanatory. Potential Pug parents should feel comfortable with the cleanliness of the breeding home.

- Is the whelping (birthing) area in an active place where the pups receive social interaction?

Often Pug mamas will find their own area to give birth, no matter what the breeder has planned. However, the pups should be set up in a place

Where social interaction is mandatory.

- Are the parents on site; how are their temperaments?

- Are the breeders knowledgeable about Pugs?

- How often do they breed their females?

Pregnancy is a taxing process that takes its toll on a Pugs health. Mamas should only breed once every three cycles and really have no more than three litters in their life.

- Were there health screens for the parents?

While this isn't necessarily a deal breaker, it is important to ask if there are any genetic defects that a Pug parent should be aware of. Pugs are medically compromised as it is (medical deficiencies are covered in chapter eight) it's best to know, up front, if the pup is predisposed to anything in particular.

Research is key when interviewing a Pug breeder. Most breeders get into the business because they are passionate about the breed. With passion comes knowledge. If they don't know much about Pugs, move along to the next breeder.

It may feel as if the breeder is assessing the potential Pug parent by asking about work, travel, or family habits. This is a good sign. It shows they care about these pups and their future home.

If something feels off about the interview, it's okay to go to the next person on the list. Not only is this a financial commitment, but an emotional one as well. The average life expectancy of a Pug is 12-15 years. That's 12-15 years of being shadowed, snuggled and depended on.

Benefits of purchasing from a reputable breeder

The pros of locating and purchasing from a respectable breeder is peace of mind.

There is comfort in knowing where the dog comes from. The environment in which it was raised during its first imprint phase (see puppy development, chapter four), some reassurance that the puppy is medically fit, and peace of mind that there is little to no emotional baggage accompanying this fur baby.

And the drawbacks

Cons would be if the breeder wasn't reputable. With a negligent breeder there is no guarantee that the puppy would be medically fit or mentally sound.

Puppy mills put on a good front. This is why it is so important to inspect the entire facility where the puppies are born and reared.

Stores of ill repute

Puppy mills often sell to pet stores. That doggy in the window didn't come from a concerned and caring breeder, she came from someone who doesn't care for the dogs they rear and can only see the amount of money they can make.

OPTION TWO- RESCUES AND SHELTERS

A huge segment of the pet loving community would never consider the possibility of purchasing from a breeder, especially when there are so many unwanted pets languishing away in shelters. Good thing Pugs often don't last long in most shelters.

Because they love everybody and are attention seekers, they get noticed more quickly than some of the other breeds that are often relinquished.

"We'd searched countless rescues and dozens of shelters for a special Pug. Stokie found us at a shelter. We were getting into the car, disappointed and still Pug-less. Stokie broke away from the volunteer walking him, jumped into the back seat of our car and sat, happily waiting to go home."

Shelter benefits

The pros of adoption from a shelter or rescue are the most obvious, providing a family for a Pug. Since Pugs thrive in a family environment, being in a shelter must be difficult for them. Most shelters/rescues work with qualified veterinarians to ensure all animals are healthy, up to date on their vaccinations, spayed/neutered and often microchipped.

Pug rescues

The difference between a shelter and a rescue is as diverse as night and day. Both are often run as non-profit organizations and rely heavily on volunteers. A shelter is often a brick and mortar facility housing animals for the public to view and visit. A rescue is usually run solely by volunteers that love a specific breed or type of dog.

Those that run Pug shelters understand the breed like no other. They will open their homes to foster unwanted Pugs. It may cause some of the foster families to become a bit protective over their charges and will do their utmost to ensure their foster Pug is going into his "furever" home.

There may be a few more hoops to jump through, home inspections and so on, but for one who truly wants to share their home with a Pug, what's a little red tape?

The downside of adoption

One of the only cons with adoption is not knowing what emotional difficulties come with the new Pug.

Thankfully, 90% of temperament issues can be solved through positive reinforcement training, lots of love, and a little bit of chicken.

OPTION THREE- IN HOUSE BREEDING

This option is not for the faint of heart, nor the weak willed. The person that begins breeding Pugs must love the breed and be mindful of upholding breed standards. They must also be cautious in their pursuits.

The female should be over the age of two and gone through at least two heat cycles. A heat cycle lasts roughly twenty-eight days. It's fairly evident when a female Pug is in heat by the vaginal discharge and the "blowing" of her coat. Pugs tend to shed quite a bit as it is, females in heat will shed more than the average Pug.

Safeguard future litters

Ensure the genetic well-being of any potential litter by getting the mother health tested before she meets her mate. Choose a stud that has a good temperament and is healthy.

Once all that is done, tests are cleared and the mating has commenced, the only thing left to do is wait. There really is no way to tell if the Pug is pregnant until the end of her term. A Pug's gestation period lasts between 60-65 days.

Labor pains

Mama will become quite lethargic towards the end of the gestation period. When labor begins, most Pugs find their own place to give birth. A human should stay close to monitor the mama, lending a hand if it turns out that the female Pug isn't the

maternal type (a lot of them aren't), not to mention
this is an exhausting process for the mama

"We hadn't planned on keeping any of the
puppies from the litter, but Bugsy wormed
his way into my heart. Bottle feeding a
puppy is quite the bonding experience."

Delivery

Because of the size of the Pugs head, there is a 50%
chance the puppies will be born via C-section. If the
mama is able to deliver naturally there are some
things a human should be prepared to do if the
mama is unable or unwilling to do it herself; clean
the amniotic sac off the puppy after it's born, deliver
the after birth, and cut the umbilical cord. Some
mama Pugs have no desire to nurse or take care of

the babies because it takes time away from their human family, this would also fall on the shoulders of the human.

Benefit of the breeder

One of the pros for this option is if the human enjoys having the pitter patter of little paws following them. An average Pug litter is three to five pups. Some accidental breeders have reported feeling a closer bond with their Pug, after going through this experience.

Shortcomings

A major con is expenses. If someone decides to go into breeding to make some extra money, they learn quickly it's not an easy few bucks. Pug mama's often need constant medical attention once they hit the final two weeks of pregnancy. Doctor's visits add up. Surgical services like a C-section are costly.

Puppies need wellness checks and vaccinations.

If the mama decides not to nurse, special puppy formula will need to be purchased.

Expenses aside, there is also the time commitment to nursing, caring for and raising a littler of pups. One of the hardest things is the emotional investment; especially if one of the pups dies. Whether it was natural or accidental, it does happen.

WORD OF CAUTION

Be wary of internet pet listings, some of them put their best foot forward to the customers, but many breeders listed on these sites are most likely puppy mills. Research, observe and trust intuition.

Sadly, there isn't only puppy mills to worry about, there are pet flippers as well. Those are the people that will acquire a dog for free or small rehoming fee and turn around to sell the dog for a higher price. Pet flippers have also been known to steal dogs from the yards of their loving families and resell them to strangers. Pugs are especially vulnerable because they're in high demand.

Chapter 4:
Bringing Up Baby

Puppies, puppies, puppies! Bring on the Puppies! Cute little balls of fluff and curiosity. Pug puppies hold their own set of unique qualities that may endear them more to their humans. What you see is what you get as far as the Pug is concerned. This chapter will cover Pug puppy stages in all their unique and uncomplicated glory.

Birth to seven weeks

This crucial period a puppy should stay with his mother and littermates. It is the time where puppies learn, grow and explore their environment. They learn to interact and become social. It is also the magical period where their personalities begin to emerge.

Unless the Pug parent is a breeder, the owner won't be around for this essential growth age. Pug puppies grow rapidly. Their birth weight triples in 8 weeks. Its normal for the puppy to sleep 18-22 hours a day. Growing up can be exhausting.

Seven to twelve weeks

This is the time most Pugs find their forever homes and begin their new life as, what the Pug community lovingly refers to as, Velcro dogs.

By seven weeks the pup has the brain capacity to learn basic training cues such as come, stay, sit and the appropriate place to go potty. She also learns through action and consequence.

The action consequence sequence also plays into the fear impact period. Between the age of eight and eleven weeks, it is crucial to introduce Pugs to new things slowly and with positive vibes. If they have a negative experience, say with a child, a stranger, or a vacuum cleaner, the imprint will most likely have a lifelong effect on the Pug.

Three to eight months:

Growing up is hardest for the parents. In this time period, Pugs, who have a predilection for being willful anyway, will test their humans by pushing boundaries. They may turn a deaf ear when called or "forget" certain cues. Positive reinforcement training is critical. Parents need to show their Pug who the leader is without breaking his spirit.

> "It took our family some time to adjust while
> Tank went through his "bratty" phase.
> Fortunately, we lived through it. Now that
> he's matured a bit, he's the best Pug I've ever
> lived with."

Eight to fourteen months:

The second imprint period happens during this phase. Puppies are still pushing boundaries, as they launch themselves into full on teenage rebellion.

Pug males are especially prone stubborn independence during this phase, until they reach maturity. A firm but fair hand is needed while raising a teenage Pug. Once adulthood has set in, the Pug that is raised with boundaries will mellow into adulthood with ease.

Don't be fooled

People who aren't familiar in the ways of the Pug may refer to the dog as dim or incapable of learning. On the contrary, Pugs are smart, independent thinkers.

Pugs need a reason to learn, or they'll poo-poo even the most gifted trainer. Since Pugs are a gluttonous bunch, high praise food treats are often used to keep his interest.

When giving treats for good behavior, offer small, bite size delicacies that doesn't require extensive chewing. Pugs love food, treats, anything yummy. They will scarf down any tasty morsel offered and may forget to chew. Small bites swallow easily; they also don't waste the time of Pug or trainer by waiting for the chomping to subside before continuing the lesson.

Adventurous pups

Training a Pug puppy requires a little patience. While most Pug adults are mellow, Velcro dogs, puppies enjoy 30 seconds of snuggle time before it's off to the next adventure. Pug puppies buzz with energy and curiosity. Pugs are naturally curious anyway, a puppy gets distracted easily.

Keep pup safe

Because of the natural inquisitive nature of the Pug, it is best to puppy proof the home. Maybe puppy proof-plus his entire living area. Tape down cords and wires to keep from being chewed; put child safety locks on the kitchen cabinet doors, they watch and may mimic the opening of a cupboard under the kitchen sink. Become aware of potential dangers, choking hazards, anything the Pug may investigate while in adventure mode.

Potty? Playtime!

Teaching a Pug to go outside for potty, may seem like an easy endeavor. Remember Pugs are people obsessed? Most can't just go outside do their business and come back in; they need human companionship out there, in all the elements; to keep them company.

Weather watch

Speaking of elements, most Pugs don't fare well in inclement weather. If it's snowing, raining, windy, or hot the pup may substitute the floor of the kitchen for the grass outside.

If there is an accident, don't rub his nose in it. Don't yell or become angry. This will only create fear and confusion. Put a leash on and take him to his potty place. Let him sniff and get used to the area. If he pees while out there, act like he performed the most amazing feat, praise him whole heartedly. If treats are handy give them freely.

Put a positive association with being outside and eliminating there. Eventually, the Pug will be okay in the elements, without his human, for the time it takes to pee.

"Groucho hates the rain, absolutely hates it! We tried everything to get him to potty outside when it rains. The only way I can get him outside when it rains is sliced banana. He turns his nose up at everything else I offer, but would probably poop outside during a blizzard if I had sliced banana on hand to give him when he was done."

To crate or not to crate

A conundrum among dog owners. Some feel that it is cruel and unusual punishment to lock a dog in a "box". Others would be bereft without theirs. Canine ancestors were den animals, using a crate is like creating a den for the dog to chill in. The Pug, however, was bred for the express purpose of being a companion dog, did they ever sleep in a den? Probably not. What's an owner to do?

Crates, when used correctly, do provide a safe place for the dog to hang out in when they are stressed, very much like having their own room. It also keeps them out of trouble when their owner isn't around. That being said, some Pugs become distressed if their human walks out of a room.

If an owner feels compelled to crate train, make sure it is a positive experience all the way around. Make the crate a fun place to be with comfy blankets, fun toys and some tasty treats like a frozen treat ball filled with peanut butter.

Pugs like to lick (and lick, and lick), by giving him a frozen treat, he can lick to his heart's content. He may be so into the treat he might not notice his human has gone. Maybe.

Leash 'em up

Most cities have some form of leash law. If not, it's best to make leash walking a habit anyway. While there are a select number of Pugs that stay close to their human and don't care to wander off, Pug puppies won't develop the layer of Velcro for at least two years. They enjoy being explorers.

Which leash?

Retractable leashes are extremely popular, but may also be dangerous. Known for causing lacerations to both dog and owner, the retractable leash also allows very little control over a hyper dog that wants to sniff everything. Best to stick with a standard 6' nylon leash.

"We acquired three sister Pugs, Goneril, Regan and Cornelia. I tried leash training them on harnesses with retractable leashes, the end result was me in the ER with a broken ankle. We kept the harnesses, but have switched to regular six foot leashes. It's just easier…"

Collar or harness?

Dogs should always wear a collar, with their identification and vaccinations tags attached. When it comes to being walked, some dogs have an issue with choking themselves while being collar led. Pugs, with their smaller palates and shortened airways should be harnessed while being walked. If the Pug is overly exuberant, the harness won't impede the breathing process, which may already be labored by the walk.

Chapter 5:
Graduating to Adulthood

The adult is more of a mellow fellow, however, there is still the clownish, attention seeking Pugish charm that win most people over.

This chapter will concentrate on the adult Pug, cover more training techniques, exercise, veterinary care, the Pugs devotion to food, and some special needs that Pugs shouldn't live without.

"Hal loves to eat. Given the opportunity, he would eat all day. His guilty pleasure is raiding the cookie jar by pushing a chair from the table to the sink, climbing up and over. He's a sneaky one, he is!"

After the age of three

Congratulations! The puppy has now become an adult, let the lounging begin. It's often easy to assume that the adult Pug is a low energy dog.

After all, she does seem to catch a lot of zzzz's during the day; only getting up to eat. This isn't healthy for any Pug, though. With their minimal desire to exercise and their avarice towards food, Pugs tend to put on weight very easily.

These paws were made for walking

It's important to get the dog off the couch and out walking. Not only is it good physical exercise, it's a good mental workout as well.

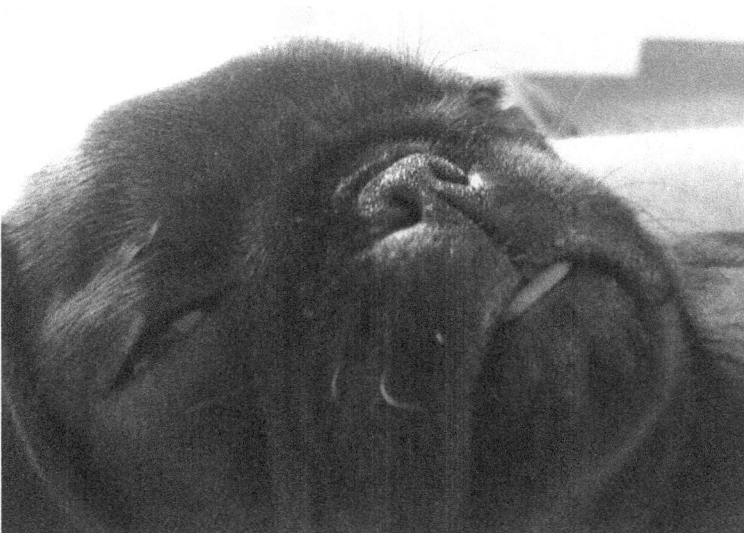

All dogs need daily mental stimulation or they will get bored. Boredom usually leads to behavioral issues and destruction. A Pug may not tear down a wall with its bare paws (that takes too much effort), but they might begin licking obsessively, which will cause hot spots to develop.

Embrace bodily functions

Pugs have short faces and large droopy jowls. Because of the jowls, they tend to drool.

Their short face forces them to gulp air when they eat, causing heinous gas emissions.

Pugs snort, wheeze, blow snot when they sneeze, rub eye bogies on the furniture, snore in their sleep, and may leave odorous anal leakage (due to unexpressed anal glands) on their owner's lap.

They require some regular hygienic care such as cleaning the folds of their face, cleaning the flaps of their ears, brushing their coat, and expressing anal glands.

Watch the food intake

It's been mentioned, but bears repeating, Pugs love to eat. They love their food as much as they love their humans, perhaps a little more than their humans.

If they can manage to reach, they are prolific table/counter surfers. Something gets dropped on the floor, it's gone. A Pug parent that manages to teach a Pug to "drop it" will quickly find that "drop it" translates into Puglish for "swallow it quickly".

Pica; the reality

There is a condition called Pica, that a fair few Pugs suffer from. Pica is when a living being eats non-food items. Some Pugs have a thing for toilet paper and Kleenex. A used tissue is considered a delicacy.

Any Pug suffering with this disorder will likely end up on the operating table with obstructed bowels.

Christmas Eve we were sitting around the tree. I saw a glass ornament in my Pug Brandi's mouth. Before I managed the "drop it" cue, there was a crunch of glass. I wrestled the dog to the ground and pulled shards out of her mouth and throat. I spent that night at the veterinary ER praying my Pug was okay (she's fine). We've now amended our Christmas decorations to accommodate Brandi's unusual tastes.

Training the adult

Some owners believe that training ends with puppyhood. This is far from accurate. Pugs need constant training, reminders, praise and more training. Pugs can be strong minded and strong willed. They will conveniently forget their name, how to sit, or how to come for the sake of trying to get the upper hand.

Mental flexing mandatory

Pugs (all dogs really) need the mental stimulation of training. Training classes are an effective means to get cerebral motivation, social interaction, and attention a Pug thrives on. Patience and persistence are needed to rear a self-confident Pug into their golden years.

Housetraining never ends (sorry!)

This is a constant source of discussion among Pug owners, "When will my Pug be house trained?" The answer varies from Pug to Pug of course, but on the whole, there may be no end to the floor puddles, unless an owner is willing to put forth some concerted effort.

Try this for indoor eliminators

One effective housetraining method is called "sitting" on the dog. This is a dream come true for the Pug, because they would literally be strapped to their human 24/7. By leashing the dog to the owner, the owner limits free range of the home, controls when the dog goes out (every 60-90 minutes), praises the dog wildly when the dog does what's expected (potties outside) and even treats the Pug. Crating at night is mandatory, but if it's possible, move the crate close to the bed so the Pug can still be close to his human.

Allergies abound

It's good to mention at this point, now that counter surfing, gluttony and Pica have been discussed, that many Pugs do have food allergies. Usually with the grains associated with most commercial dog foods. Chapter seven will focus solely on food, food allergies and dietary needs of Pugs.

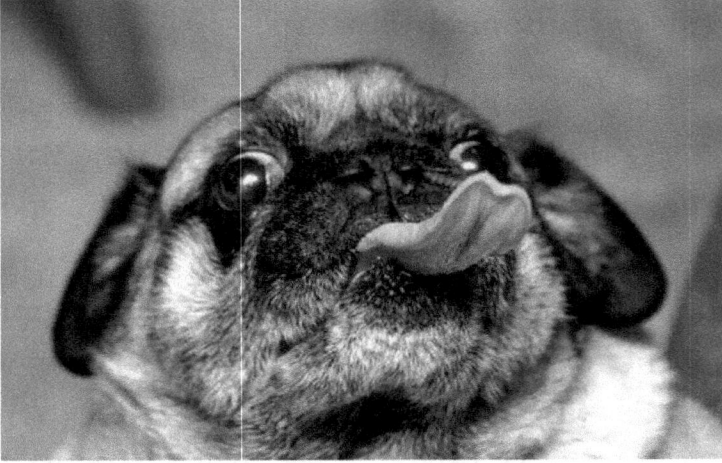

We had no idea when we adopted Maisie that she was allergic to everything. No exaggeration!

Through trial and many, many, many errors we finally found the right shampoo, the right dog food and the right bedding (She's allergic to cotton fabric…

Shedding woes

Pugs shed, a lot. It comes as a surprise to most first time Pug parents as to just how much these short haired dogs shed. Brushing out the coat is essential for keeping the shedding to a minimum. Using a soft bristle brush first stroke with the hair, then against the hair.

Washing the Pug

Bathing should be kept to a minimum to keep from drying out the dog's skin. Usually once a month or so. Shampoo and condition the Pug's coat. Steer clear of washing the head and face in the bath. Water in the ear folds will cause infection.

Facial care

Clean the facial folds with an unscented baby wipe or a moist towel often. For those Pugs with extreme wrinkles this should be done daily. Make sure to dry the folds after they've been wiped down to minimize the occurrence of fungus or infection.

Check and clean the Pugs ears often with a moist cotton ball or wipe. Ears are prone to wax build up, yeast infection and ear mites.

The nose has a tendency to develop a layer of dried gunk across it. The medical term is nasodigital hyperkeratosis; translation should read "nose crud". It can be taken care of with a little Vaseline or an unscented aloe/vitamin E lotion. Check with the vet on recommendations.

Anal expressions

Let's talk about the butt for a moment, more specifically the dread anal sacs. These are pockets of flesh around the anus that fill with fluid. A Pug's anal sac tend to fill quickly and need to be expressed often.

A Pug lets people know his anal sacs are full by scooting his butt along the carpet like his rear is on fire.

While it's easier (and less caustic for the owner) to have the vet or groomer express them, it can add up.

Even if the owner has no intention of ever expressing anal sacs, it's best to learn how to do this, just in case.

Chapter 6:
The Golden Years
(Caring for the Senior Pug)

Usually around the age of nine or so, a Pug will be considered a senior. A Pug parent may notice a little gray around the face, move a little slower and be less enthused about her daily walk. Care, responsibilities, medical issues, these are all things that will be altered to ensure the Pug will enjoy her golden years with ease.

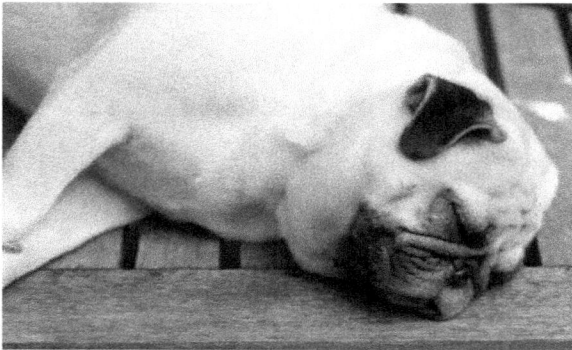

"Blowsy has such a sweet disposition, she's really has been great with my kids, even when they were toddlers. We've lived with her for twelve years. Now she is blind but it hasn't changed her a bit...she is as wonderful as

Medical check ups

Normal, bi-annual trips to the vet include geriatric testing for the senior. These screenings are done according to the dog's history and may include an EKG and additional blood work ups, included in the regular physical exam.

In between visits, vets ask Pug parents to watch for indicators of medical trouble such as

- unexplained weight loss

- a sudden increase or decrease in eating habits may indicate diabetes.

- Coughing or excessive panting may be heart trouble. Behavioral changes should also be discussed with the vet.

Exercise

The dog's had a long life and is tired, but that doesn't mean exercise should be ruled out. Pugs still need exercise to keep the heart, lungs, circulation, and joints in working order.

Watch the Pug for signs of exertion, a droopy head or tail, inability to catch her breath, limping. While she needs the exercise, she may not be able to walk her usual 10 block radius.

It's best to exercise the senior before she eats and wait at least thirty minutes after her walk before feeding her.

Plan walks accordingly. If it's supposed to be a scorcher of a day, walk in the early morning when it's cool. If a cold front is rolling in, plan on some form of exercise indoors.

Grooming

As Pugs age, their circulation slows a bit. It may take her longer to warm up after a bath. Keep extra towels handy to help her warm up. A good fifteen-minute brush everyday will keep her coat and skin healthy. It's also a good way to look for sores that aren't healing, lumps and bumps that shouldn't be there.

Behavioral issues

Even the most well-adjusted Pug may develop some behavioral issues as she gets older. These senior moments may include

- An escalation in barking, often due to hearing loss

- An increase in noise sensitivity

- An upswing in aggression, likely due to pain

- Disorientation and confusion

- Walking in circles, barking at nothing

These issues should be mentioned to the vet. Serious ailments often mask themselves in lesser symptoms.

When to see the vet

If an owner notices a personality change in their senior Pug, it's best to have the dog checked out by their veterinarian. This is to rule out any medical condition the Pug may have developed.

Sudden onset of aggression could mean the dog is in pain, medication may be necessary to get the Pug back to their old, snuggly self.

Nerve Degeneration

No one seems to know why Pugs are prone to nerve degeneration, but it is something to keep an eye out for. Symptoms of nerve degeneration include dragging the back feet, an inability to jump up and down off furniture and staggering. Incontinence is likely with this disease. Some Pug parents find a doggie wheelchair helps with mobility issues.

Dental Hygiene

It is imperative to keep up with good dental hygiene in a Pugs golden years. Keeping a regular brushing schedule may stave off several diseases that plague the heart, liver and kidneys.

When Bruce passed away I was devastated. I knew it was coming, but still wasn't prepared for the inevitable. Luckily I have some really good friends, Pug people. They hosted a wake for Bruce that had all his favorite (people) foods and music. He would have loved the party thrown for him.

Chapter 7:
A Pugs First Love (Food Facts)

It's been established that Pugs are quite unique, with appealing quirks and a charm all their own. This special brand of Puggy charm extends into their dietary habits. Some Pugs fair well on eating whatever they please, with no intestinal ramifications, others need a good parent that watches every morsel of food that goes into their mouth.

There is a lot of discussion among the Pug community as to the best course of action where feeding Pugs are concerned, it all boils down to the individual Pug. Finding what is nutritionally best for them is trial and error.

Jabba does okay with his Pug formulated kibble, but what he really wants for dinner is pizza.

Commercial Brands

Sadly, there is no "one brand fits all" type of dog food. This has never been truer than where a Pug is concerned. While a Pug can (and will) eat almost anything, it doesn't mean that they should.

Fillers a no-no

Most of the inexpensive commercial brands contain grain fillers such as corn meal, gluten meal, and/or various flours.

Because of the Pugs inherited genetics, they often find themselves with moderate to severe food allergies. The food they're most allergic to tend to be the fillers in most commercial dog food.

For the health conscious Pug, these added ingredients may cause weight gain, intestinal distress, ear infections, and skin irritation.

Labeling confusion

Read ingredient labels and dietary percentages carefully. Look for the dreaded fillers and where they are ranked in ingredient order.

If the first three or four ingredients listed are fillers (corn meal, gluten meal, flours) move along to the next brand, these most likely would disagree with a Pug's sensitive system.

Meat byproducts are ground up left overs such as internal organs (heart, liver, intestines, etc.) Meat, most often in the form of chicken, beef or lamb, or meat byproducts should be listed first on the ingredient list.

Keep in mind

Some of the higher end commercial brands come grain free and there are a few brands that promote a recipe specifically formulated for Pugs. Dry and wet options are available, depending on one's lifestyle.

Sydney LOVES watermelon. As soon as he sees one enter the house, he's immediately up on his hind legs whining for his fair share!

Raw Food Options

There are a fair few Pug parents that love the idea of feeding their Pug a raw food diet. They take comfort in knowing exactly what their dog is eating.

Benefits to a raw diet

Most owners that switch to a raw diet have found dramatic increases in their Pugs health

- clearing of fungal and yeast infections,

- reduction in skin irritation,

- lessening of external bodily fluids

 (eye goop, snotty noses, etc.)

- glossy coat,

- more energy

- cleaner teeth

 (resulting in nicer breath)

Raw treats

Oh treats! Pugs love treats! Parents have found treating a Pug is the best way to get through training. On a raw diet, treating can be as easy as chopping an apple, peeling a banana or rolling a blueberry in the direction of a Pug.

The following list of fruits are Pug approved and full of vitamins, fiber, potassium and other trace minerals essential to keep a growing dog healthy.

- Apples

- Bananas

- Blueberries

- Blackberries

- Raspberries

- Cranberries help clear UTI's (urinary tract infections)

- Strawberries

- Kiwis

- Pears are good for loosening up constipation

- Watermelon (Steer clear of the rinds and seeds though)

- Cantaloupe

- Oranges

- Pumpkin is recommended for both loosening constipation and firming up diarrhea A real two for one.

There are a number of raw, packaged treats available on the market. Most in the form of meat jerky, which most Pugs gobble up. If an owner has a food dehydrator, they might want to try their hand at making their own jerky.

The B.A.R.F. diet

The B.A.R.F. plan (Biologically Appropriated Raw Food) appears to be the most popular. It requires a balanced meal of 60-80% raw meat bones and 20-40% fruits, veggies, dairy, eggs and meat. Suggested meat is everything from beef, chicken, turkey, lamb and organ meats. The meat should be pasteurized. This will reduce the chances of bacterial growth in the meat.

Drawbacks of a raw diet

Before running out and purchasing a side of beef, however, let's discuss the downside of this option. It can get pretty expensive. A raw food diet consisting of an equal balance of meat, dairy and fruits/vegetables digest quickly. Most Pugs on this eating plan require three meals a day.

Possible bacterial infection

Even with pasteurized meat there is still the risk of bacteria associated with this diet. E. Coli, salmonella, and listeria are all suspect when dealing with raw meats. The risk to a dog is relatively low, due to their reduced and more acidic digestion period. Pug parents are the ones at a higher risk for a food borne illness.

Occasionally a tooth may be broken on a particularly tasty bone. Bone chewing also presents a choking hazard.

Due to the risk of bacterial ingestion and possible choking hazards, it is never a good idea to feed a puppy or a nursing mama raw food.

This may sound weird, but after switching Paco's diet from commercial to raw; not only did I notice the shinier coat, fresher breath, and dramatic decrease in eye bogies but he seemed to sleep sounder and snore less. Or maybe I've just gotten used to the snoring.

Home cooked meals

As with the raw food eating plan, cooking meals for the Pug gives the owners more control over what their dog eats. They know exactly what is going into the prepared food, which cuts down on allergies and weight gain.

It also allows the Pug parent a small sense of relief when commercial dog food recalls are announced.

Things to consider

Before revamping the kitchen into a Pug diner, talk with the vet about calories and nutritional balance. It is easy to cook for a dog, but without proper dietary guidance, cooking for a Pug could result in an increase of medical issues and an increase in weight.

Well balanced meal

A healthy Pug meal often consists of 50% meat, 25% fruits/veggies, and 25% of grains. Even with a healthy balance and a strict, detailed menu, the dog may lose out on necessary nutrients. Talk with the vet about supplements to keep the Pug healthy and active far into his golden years.

The home cooked plan is almost as expensive as the raw food plan. Meals need to be planned out, ingredients need to be purchased fresh.

It is time consuming to prepare three meals a day for the dog. Everything may be prepared in the morning, but there is the risk of bacterial growth if the food is cooled down too fast, or sits out too long while cooling. Meals shouldn't be more than two days old.

Supplements

A Pug's diet may not be as balanced as it should be, the commercial kibble isn't supplying the right nutrients, the dog needs a little extra to keep him going. Supplements are a good way to keep a Pug healthy. It's best to consult with a veterinarian before administering any supplement. Especially with a Pug, considering their genetic predisposition to allergies.

Canine Glucosamine

Chondroitin occurs naturally in a dog's cartilage. A glucosamine supplement will improve on the joints flexibility and reduce swelling caused by arthritis. It keeps the joints healthy, which is good for the Pug that is predisposed to hip dysplasia. Glucosamine come in both pill and soft chew form. An owner may find these supplements at a local pet store or through their veterinarian.

Omega-3

Fish oil aids digestion and gives the coat a healthy shine. Some Pug parents even report a reduction in shedding, however that hasn't been confirmed through research. It most often is given in liquid form, squeezed over the Pugs food. 20mg of EPA/DHA blend daily is often sufficient.

For those owners concerned about fish toxicity, coconut oil is an alternative to fish oil. It still contains the omega-3's a Pug needs for optimum health.

Omega-3, found in fish and coconut oil is excellent for keeping inflammation to a minimum. However, flooding a Pug's body with too much Omega-3 can cause inflammation and with it a host of medical conditions. Check with the vet on how many Omega-3's a Pug should be getting.

> The vet said sardines are a good source of omegas for my Pug. One sardine gets hidden in her food bowl couple times a week. Clancy was fond of her kibble before, but now she does a little jig when she smells the sardines.

Vitamin B-12

Pugs on a raw food diet won't have a vitamin B-12 deficiency, since it's found primarily in meat. Vitamin B-12 aids the nervous system, is needed for cell growth and keeps up a Pugs energy level.

Vitamin C

Aids in increasing the immune system and also helps in cartilage and joint repair. There are supplements available that combine glucosamine and vitamin C. Combined a Pugs joints should be well protected against deterioration.

Brewer's yeast

Containing most of the B vitamins (to convert food into energy), chromium (good for regulating blood sugar), and the antioxidant selenium (promotes healthy cell growth), Brewer's yeast is whispered to also repel fleas, keeps a Pug coat shiny and reduces shedding. If the Pug suffers from allergies to yeast, best steer clear of this supplement.

Linoleic Acid

Another Omega fatty acid (this time 6) is needed for healthy skin and fur. Found in certain oils, such as sunflower, linoleic fatty acid prevents dry, itchy, scaly skin and dull coats.

Bromelain

Extracted from the pineapple, bromelain is an anti-inflammatory supplement. Often given to Pugs that suffer from arthritis and other joint issues, this supplement is also regarded as a natural histamine. Pugs suffering from allergies and sinus issues may benefit from this natural source.

Words of caution

Switching food

Above and beyond anything else, it's the Pugs health that is most important. What works best for the Pug and the parent?

If there is the possibility switching over from one feeding method to another, begin gradually. Switching food abruptly (even going from one commercial brand to another commercial brand) could cause major dietary distress. Add the new food to the old, increasing by ¼ cup each day. Watch for signs of allergic reaction, dietary distress, or flat out Pug rejection.

Bloat

Gastric volvulus, also known as bloat, occurs when a dog's stomach fills with food, fluid or gas making it expand. Bloat comes on suddenly with little warning. It should be treated quickly before it becomes life threatening.

Signs a Pug suffers from bloat may include a swollen stomach, attempts to vomit with nothing coming up, anxiety, acting restless and/or drooling (more than a normal Pug would).

If the condition worsens the Pug may have pale gums, a rapid heartbeat, collapse, or be short of breath.

Pugs are more susceptible to bloat due to their love of scarfing food quickly and eating too much at one time.

The only course of treatment is through a veterinarian's office. The vet will need to relieve the pressure in the Pugs tummy either by tube of needle.

I had no idea that Pugs were prone to bloat, thought that was a big dog issue. Until Farley came down with it. After all the conflicting information we received on how to avoid Bloat, we use the old tennis ball in bowl trick to slow her eating a bit.

Foods to avoid

In keeping in line with most Pug's allergies to fillers and grains, an owner should avoid feeding their Pug (or any dog) chocolate. Chocolate contains theobromine and caffeine, both which can be toxic to dogs. The darker the chocolate, the higher the toxicity.

The artificial sweetener, Xylitol is also highly toxic to dogs and should not be fed to them under any circumstances.

Grapes and raisins have been shown to cause kidney failure.

Nuts may cause tremors, vomiting and pancreatitis.

Onions and garlic could possibly lead to gastrointestinal distress and damage red blood cells.

Rawhide chews are dangerous for Pugs. In their gluttonous haze of euphoric gnawing, there is the possibility of ripping off a chunk and choking.

Chapter 8:
A High Maintenance Breed
(medically speaking)

Pugs are popular, wildly popular. Because of the high demand for these playful pups, they have been overbred and inbred, creating a host of genetic disorders.

In addition to the genetic disorders listed throughout the chapter most Pugs suffer from one or more of the following

- breathing difficulties

- passing out due to a lack of oxygen

- high blood pressure

- disrupted sleep from constant snoring

- facial skin fold infections

- severe eye problems

- cataracts

- scratched corneas

- excessive flatulence due to gulping and swallowing of air while eating or drinking

- difficulty walking

- vaccination sensitivity

Brachycephalic Syndrome

Put in layman's terms, the Pug has a cute, flat, squished face. While this may look appealing, it does cause breathing issues.

Brachycephalic translates into "short headed". Most owners dismiss a majority of the symptoms of brachycephalic syndrome as the norm for Pugs. These overlooked symptoms are high pitched wheezing, excessive panting, sleeping with a toy in the mouth for easier breathing, sleep apnea, reluctance to exercise, intolerance to the heat, snorting or gagging.

Reverse Sneezing

Most Brachycephalic breeds suffer from a condition called "reverse sneezing". Instead of blowing the irritants out as with a regular sneeze, the soft palate tends to spasm with an irritation. Nasal passages constrict and airways can't blow anything out, or breathe anything in. Eventually the passages right themselves and life goes on.

The reverse sneezing itself isn't cause for concern, however, it may lead to severe issues such as breathing difficulties and nosebleeds.

Reverse sneezing may occur due to a sensitivity to allergens in the air, eating or drinking too fast, sinus infections, or collar pulling while leash walking.

Stenotic Nares

That's a relatively snazzy name for closed nostrils. It's a genetic disorder, associated with brachycephalic syndrome. The nostrils could be partially or fully closed to earn this distinction. Most Pugs suffering from stenotic nares are born this way.

It can be treated with surgery if it is found the Pug isn't getting enough oxygen.

Luxating Patella

Imagine the Pug romping in the grass, minding his own business, loving life and suddenly he yelps in pain. He'll most likely pull his hind leg in close and hobble for 10-15 minutes before setting the leg back down and resume his joyful countenance. What just happened? A Luxating Patella (Trick Knee) has struck.

This trick of the knee is no fun. The patella, which is normally set in a grooved pocket at the top of the femur shifts and moves, causing the Pug extreme discomfort. It may happen once every couple of months, but as the dog gets older it will probably occur with more frequency. Surgery is the most effective way to correct the issue.

Legg-Perthes Disease

A disorder involving the hip joint, Legg-Perthes disease occurs when the blood supply to the top of the leg bone (femur) decreases. This will cause the hip joint to disintegrate.

Often occurring when a puppy is between 4 – 6 months old. The leg will lose its function and begin to atrophy. Surgery is the most common fix.

Distichiasis

This syndrome occurs when the eyelashes grow apart from the eyelid. Distichiasis causes the unnecessary lashes to scratch the protruding eye, which leads to corneal ulcers and Pigmentary Keratitis. Surgery is needed to remove the extra hairs. During surgery the veterinarian may apply heat or freeze the eyelid to cauterize the surface, preventing this condition from occurring in the future.

Entropion

A medical term for rolling of the eyelid. Often it is the lower lid closest to the nose. This condition may lead to Pigmentary Keratitis and should be corrected with surgery. It is genetic. Pugs born with this condition should not breed. It will be passed along to future generations.

Pigmentary Keratitis

A Pugs eyes are very prominent, it's one of the first things people notice. Because of the prominence, a Pugs eyes are prone to several ocular issues including Pigmentary Keratitis.

This disease occurs when the brown pigment in the eye begins to grow over the cornea, eventually blinding the dog. Eye drops have been developed to slow the pigmentation growth, but there is no cure.

> When my Oda Mae first lost her sight, she'd wander around the house looking for me. I put jingle bells on my shoes so she could always find me, no matter where I was.

Hip/Elbow Dysplasia

According to the veterinary orthopedic foundation, on a list of 142 breeds, Pugs are number 2 when it comes to suffering from hip/elbow dysplasia. It is estimated that one out of every two Pugs will be diagnosed with hip or elbow dysplasia.

Dysplasia is described as an abnormal formation of the hip/elbow socket. They deteriorate gradually, eventually causing severe arthritis, lameness, and eventual loss of function in the hip or elbow.

The condition may occur due to genetics, a lifetime of poor nutrition and obesity or strenuous exercise at too early an age.

There are several ways to treat dysplasia, depending on the severity of the condition. There are many surgical options and also non-surgical treatments. Non-surgical treatments include a variety of anti-inflammatory medications, diet, supplements and physical therapy. Since dysplasia is genetic there is no means of prevention.

Pyoderma

Skin infections aren't fun to begin with. Pyoderma occurs when the Pugs skin gets infected. Often it presents itself as skin sacs full of thick white pus. If the infection moves into the folds of the dogs skin it will become red and moist with an unpleasant stench. In most cases a veterinarian will prescribe an antibacterial cream. Inspecting the Pugs skin regularly often (but not always) keeps skin irritants to a minimum.

Cheyletiella Dermatitis

Otherwise known as "walking dandruff" this condition is caused by miniscule mites. If a Pug has heavy dandruff, particularly located down the middle of his back, contact the vet to have it treated. These mites are contagious and will spread to other pets in the home.

Hemivertebrae

That cute, curly, little corkscrew tail may be the reason for a Pug to suffer from the condition known as hemivertebrae, a tongue twisting word indicating a deformity of one or more vertebrae in the spine. This can lead to pain, inability to walk with the hind legs and incontinence. Some Pug owners have raved over the combination of water therapy and physical therapy to get the Pug the exercise they need.

Pug Dog Encephalitis

This neurological disorder is only found in Pugs and is often fatal. No one seems to know what brings on this particular strain of encephalitis. Research has indicated it may be genetic, but there are no conclusive findings. It often comes on between 2-3 years of age. Indications a Pug is suffering with encephalitis may include behavioral changes, seizures, pressing their head against walls or objects, disorientation, or walking in circles to name a few. The disease progresses rapidly (often within days). Contact the vet immediately as soon as symptoms occur.

Idiopathic Epilepsy

Encephalitis isn't the only seizure producing disorder that Pugs suffer from. Idiopathic Epilepsy bring on seizures in Pugs, but there is no rhyme or reason for the seizures, they just occur. It's best to bring the Pug into the vet for a checkup after a seizure to rule out any other medical condition.

Pugs overheat easily. We learned that one the hard way when Zep was a puppy. Our morning walk started later than usual. When we got home the sun was and the temp were high. Zep keeled over as soon as we walked over the threshold, Thankfully, we cooled him down and got some water into him. Not making that mistake again.

Chapter 9:
Pug Approved Activities

Don't be fooled by the couch potato attitude and the lack of interest in game play, the Pug loves (needs) mental stimulation to maintain their health and well-being. Without mental stimulation (as mentioned in previous chapters) a Pug will get bored. A bored Pug will make life very unpleasant for her family.

Walks are great for a little mental flexing, it allows the Pug to enter a new area, read the dog "mail" (sniffing to see what canine has come by and left their mark). This however isn't enough to exercise that smart brain of theirs. Not only do these suggestions offer mental stimulation, they also provide bonding time between human and Pug.

OBEDIENCE TRAINING

All dogs should go through (and maintain) basic obedience training. Basic training consists of the standard cues; sit, stay, down, up, heel, etc.

Advanced obedience training makes the basics a little more challenging. Advanced training teaches a Pug how to focus on her owner while there are so many distractions going on around them.

Canine Good Citizen (CGC) Training is not for the faint of heart, but Pugs seem to excel. In a CGC program a Pug will learn how to be a model dog.

This training program lays the foundation for agility training, performance events and for the special Pug, becoming a therapy dog.

Any of these classes may be taught privately or in a classroom setting. Interview the trainer first before signing up for anything. Not all trainers work the same, find one that shares the owner's philosophy and understands a Pugs unique charm.

Agility

The sport of agility is to train a dog to run through an obstacle course. Courses vary greatly. A dog may be expected to run through tunnels, jump hurdles, climb towers, or teeter on a table.

Pugs aren't athletes, that's been established. However, is there another sport that a Pug would be better at? Agility requires a dog to be completely and solely focused on their handler.

Training for agility is a fun way for both Pug and parent to get some exercise. It is also a good bonding experience. Most dog training facilities offer agility classes.

The Shell Game

Where's the treat? Find the treat. Is this the treat?

Sit on the floor with three identical plastic cups. The cups shouldn't be see through. Sit the Pug opposite of the dealer and show him the treat. Put the treat under one of the cups, shuffle the cups around on the floor and give the cue "Find the treat".

At first the Pug will most likely knock the cups over with his nose and gobble up the tasty morsel. Once he gets the hang of the game, the human can start teaching manners and restraint by implementing training cues.

"Leave it" and "Take it" are handy tools to keep any owners training arsenal.

Dog Shows

Pugs are always popular at the dog shows. Most clubs adhere to the breed standard and some of more liberal clubs allow neutered dogs into the competition.

Before stepping into that show ring, however, there are a couple things to ensure the best Pug wins.

- Pugs should go through advanced obedience, if not CGC training. It's required to put their best paw forward; judges look for good temperament.

This will satisfy not only the physical act of trotting around a ring, but the mental aspect having to remember her training.

- Check the breed standard guidelines. Especially in a conformity competition. There is a long list of how to determine whether a Pug is "Show" quality or merely "Pet" quality

Being a show dog will also fulfill the social needs of a Pug, the attention seeking requirement as well.

Breed standard is what judges look at when judging the Pug. If the standards aren't met, then the dog will not be allowed to compete.

Judges look for a well-proportioned body with hard muscles. They also expect a pleasant temperament with a lively attitude.

The Kennel Club and its American counterpart, the American Kennel Club both have an extensive list of what is considered breed standard for a Pug.

The Pug is considered a toy breed. Weighing in between 15-18 pounds, standing 10 inches in height (at the shoulder) they are considered the largest in their class.

Only one Pug has ever won "Best in Show" at the Westminster Kennel Dog Club Show. In 1981 a Pug nicknamed "Chuckie" beat out close to 3,000 other dogs to walk away with the coveted title.

Hide and Seek

As the name indicates, the owner could hide anything; a treat, a ball, a toy or even himself.

The Pug will enjoy hunting for the treasure. Start simple by putting the Pug in sit/stay. Let her see where the object is, put a towel over it and release her to find the object. Attach a cue to it such as "Find it".

Do this a couple of times until she gets the hang of it. Find a different hiding spot and start again. Eventually the owner will hide the object out of the Pug's line of vision. Give her the verbal cue to go hunt for the item…(making sure of course it's not the CAT…)

Dancing Queens (and Kings)

Let's recap, Pugs love their people, check. Pugs love attention, check. Pugs love cutting up to get that attention, check. Then maybe this Pug is ready for the dance floor. There are several national and international dance organizations where guardian and Pug can strut their sweet moves in front of hundreds of people.

No strict standards to adhere to, follow the beat of the music to Funkytown. Or better yet some freestyle music training classes. The Pug may be a natural born dancer; can the owner keep up?

Our Pug, Paisley learned to skateboard by accident, by climbing up onto the board and the kids pushed her around. Soon she figured it out how to push herself and barks happily, as she tries to keep up with the kids in the neighborhood.

Hidden Talents

Pugs are smart, when they want to learn something they'll find a way to retain the information. There isn't anything these Pugs can't do for the right parent.

Some Pugs have an aversion to water, others can't seem to stay out of it. These particular Pugs participate in surfing and dock diving competitions. The sky is the limit if the Pug and owner are willing and healthy.

Chapter 10:
Broaden the circle

Twenty years ago a Pug was merely another dog. He was brought into the family and expected to adjust. Now there are a myriad of business in place to help the average Pug parent get through any phase of Pug's exuberant existence.

Veterinary care

Veterinarians are no longer just "animal doctors". Now they seem to specialize in species or breed. Some veterinarians choose to take a more holistic approach to Pug care as opposed to the traditional path.

When searching for a veterinarian, decide what's most important and make a list. Here are a few ideas to get started.

- Pug knowledge

How important is it to have a vet that speaks "Puglish"?

- Rotating doctors

Most veterinary practices incorporate a team of doctors. How important is it to see the same face every visit?

- Licensed vet techs

There are some animal care places that employ qualified, unlicensed veterinary technicians. Is this a deal breaker?

Ask friends and family members about their experiences. The American Animal Hospital Association lists accredited vets on their site.

Call for an appointment without the Pug. Check out the cleanliness of the facility, talk to the staff, ask about overnight monitoring. This is just one of many times in a Pugs life a guardian needs to listen to their intuition.

Trainers

Finding a certified, experienced dog trainer is often times like digging for a needle in a haystack. Anyone can watch a couple of YouTube videos and promote themselves as a trainer or behaviorist. An owner needs to be a little savvy when interviewing trainers. A couple of things to watch for when interviewing trainers.

- Does the trainer interact with the owner, the dog or both?

While it's great the trainer loves dogs, she should be training the owner, to train the dog. If her training isn't clear to the owner, it's the Pug that won't see the need for all this hullabaloo.

- Is the trainer breed knowledgeable?

It's the trainer's job to know the breed he's working with. Yes, every dog is an individual, but a working knowledge of how the average Pug's brain works goes a very long way.

In the end it will be up to the Pug parent and their pesky intuition to decide whether they can work with a particular trainer. Finding a good match may take a couple weeks of digging through the haystack, eventually gold will be struck.

We thought we knew all about dog training, until Frankie came to live with us. We must have worked with a dozen trainers before we found one that understood Frankie's quirky nature and used it to our advantage

Groomers

Pug parents take care of the day to day cleaning of facial folds, ear flaps, brushing and nose crud. Occasionally, it's nice to have someone else bathe the dog, trim their nails, express their anal glands (an owner could be so lucky to find a groomer that's willing and able to do this.)

Another advantage to having a monthly grooming session, it's better to have an extra set of eyes. Groomers are trained in skin care; lumps, bumps and sores are more likely to be caught by the professional that the owner.

Some owners are perfectly content to trot their Pugs over to the local big box pet store, leave the dog for the afternoon and pick them up later. Others would rather find a boutique groomer that can get to know the Pug.

When deciding on a groomer, number one on the list is cleanliness. How clean is the facility? Floors swept? How does it smell? Where are the dogs kept while waiting for their appointment?

Our dog walker has become part of the family. We'd be lost (and up to our ears in yuck) without her!!!

Dog Walker

Hiring a dog walker is not the extravagant expense it used to be. Adults work, kids go to school, Pug is left alone for eight hours a day. It helps to have an extra set of legs to not only break up the monotony of the dog's day, but give him a chance to stretch his legs (and empty his bladder)

Finding a dog walker is a fairly simple process. There are professionals that earn their living from walking dogs, taking them on hikes, exercising them during the day. Some teens would rather walk a dog than babysit to earn some extra money. Ask around.

Invite the prospects over, have them meet the dog. Watch the interaction. Ask for references.

Chapter 11:
(Not so) endearing behavior issues

Throughout this book it's been stressed, hinted at, implied and stated clearly that Pugs love their humans. Utter devotion is often used to describe the Pugs endless need to find and follow their person.

This chapter will take a closer look at some of the other more eccentric quirks of the Pug. Some of these traits may be resolved with ease, others require professional help.

Social dining

Some Pugs hate dining alone. They will ignore their food, may even refuse to drink unless their person is in their personal space.

If the dog has food out all day, the Pug may grab a few pieces of kibble and bring it into another room, where people are, to eat.

Some Pugs carry their food bowl around until their person stops before setting it down to eat.

Social dining such as this, is considered a form of separation anxiety. The Pug is too stressed to eat alone. He will wait until someone is around to gulp down his meal, before being left alone again.

Easing a Pugs dining anxiety is fairly simple. Put him on a schedule. Switch from free range eating (food being out all day) to regulated meals. Guardians should schedule Pug meals around their own eating times, everyone eats together.

We're not quite sure when Miss Puggy's protective stance towards me went from cute to alarming. Needless to say, we sought help immediately. Now my husband can kiss me without fear of being

Resource guarding

On the other side of social dining anxiety, there is resource guarding. This is a common condition where a Pug loves his food, toys or other prized possessions so much that he won't let anyone near it. He'll growl, snarl, even bite to ensure his precious won't be taken away.

Resource guarding looks scary and if not treated correctly could manifest into something more. It's rumored that Josephine Bonaparte's Pug Fortune, snapped and snarled at Napoleon when the leader tried to climb into bed with his wife. Cute story or cautionary tale concerning resource guarding?

A few training tips may cure a potential guarder from turning to the dark side. Learning cues such as "Drop it" and "Leave it" may deter a Pug from prizing something too much.

Approach a Pug's food bowl while the dog eats. Drop a yummy treat into the bowl. This is telling the Pug that humans entering their space is a good thing.

A Pug with a history of resource guarding, especially if there's been an injury, should work with a professional behaviorist. Resource guarding must be dealt with swiftly and with confidence, before someone is hurt.

Separation Anxiety

Separation anxiety ranges from mild whining to total annihilation of a house. It was joked earlier that Pugs don't usually exert that kind of energy, it has been known to happen. Anxiety in Pugs is completely real, especially considering how obsessed most are with their humans.

Try this for anxiety

There are natural anxiety remedies in pet stores to ease a Pugs nerves. Soothing music, the scent of lavender and a high valued toy like a frozen peanut butter filled food ball may soothe an anxious Pug while the owner steps out. For severe cases of separation anxiety, consult a professional, certified dog trainer.

Willful Snarkiness

A Pug going through the "teen years" (18 months to three years) may exert a fair amount of boundary pushing or develop a severe case of selective hearing disorder. If trained with a firm, loving, respectful hand a Pug will grow out of this phase.

An adult Pug displaying these attributes still needs a firm, loving and respectful hand to guide him, but will also need to learn who wears the pants in the pack.

> We adopted Andi from a rescue. A week into our adjustment period, Andi began acting out. We tried to placate her, being in a new environment and all. Her attitude just got worse. Thankfully the rescue recommended a trainer who is well versed in Pug. She taught us some pack leader exercises to regain a little control in what we were regarding as Andi's kingdom.

Pack leader mentality

A family or "pack" should have clear leaders. Occasionally a head strong dog, will try to fill that role. This is when the humans need to kindly remind the Pug who is in charge. Starting with the food.

Because Pugs enjoy their food, it needs to be established who controls the food. Pack leaders feed the dog, give the dog treats, take the food away when mealtime is over.

Meals should be scheduled around the rest of the pack's meals. Pack leader eats first (just a few bites of something at the counter).

Place the Pug in a sit/stay and wait. When all eyes are on the pack leader, lower the food bowl down. If the Pug breaks the cue before being released, pick the food up and start again. When the bowl is on the ground, the leader releases the dog from sit so he can eat.

Pugs are stubborn, but they aren't stupid. They're quick to realize if they want to eat, they need to wait until the pack leader gives the release cue.

A Pug Farewell

Pugs are cute, quirky, stubborn, goofy, loveable, and have stalker like tendencies (remember all the Velcro dog references?).

In addition to their quirky nature and Puggish charm, they are considered a high maintenance breed. A host of medical conditions and the daily hygiene requirements takes Pug ownership to a new level of obligation.

Not to be left on the couch, Pugs have proven themselves to be formidable opponents in any activity they participate in. Although their penchant for breathing problems keeps them from running cross country marathons, it doesn't preclude them from getting out and having some fun on the field.

Their noble history still reigns in the present day. Pugs were bred as companion animals. They were intended to sit in the laps of royalty. Today they worship their humans, treating them as royalty. As long as there is a lap to curl up in.

Dog ownership requires commitment, Pug ownership demands dedication. With their medical issues, hygiene requirements and nutritional needs, Pugs deserve a parent that knows what they're getting into and is passionate about the responsibilities of living with a Pug.

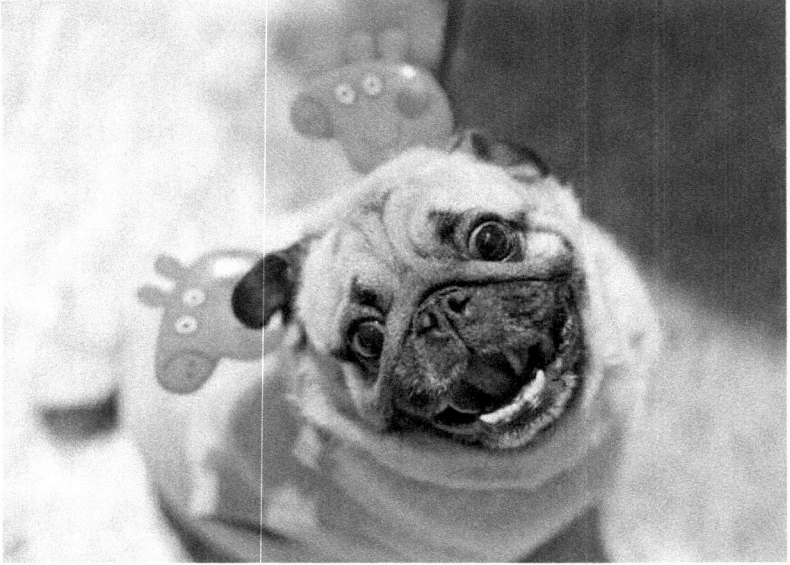

Living with a Pug is a truly unique and rewarding experience.

A

adoption · 31
Agility · 2, 76, 77
Allergies · 46
anal sacs · 49

B

behavior issues · 90
Bloat · 67
Brachycephalic Syndrome · 2, 69
Breeding · 1, 33

C

Canine Good Citizen · 76, 103
Certified Trainer · 103
Cheyletiella Dermatitis · 74
commercial dog food · 55, 62
crate train · 38

D

Dog Show · 3, 78
Dog Walker · 3, 88
Duke and Duchess of Windsor · 14

E

Ears · 48
Encephalitis · 2, 75, 76
Epilepsy · 2, 76
exercise · 39, 40, 49, 50, 69, 74, 75, 77
Exercise · 49

Index

F

facial folds · 48, 87
Freemasonry · 16

G

groomer · 49, 87
Grooming · 50

H

harness · 40
Hemivertebrae · 75
Home cooked · 1, 61

I

Imprint Phase · 104

L

Labeling confusion · 55
Leash training · 40
Legg-Perthes Disease · 2, 71
licking · 41, 104
Luxating Patella · 2, 70, 71

M

mental stimulation · 41, 45, 75

O

Obedience Training · 2, 75

GLOSSARY

American Kennel Club

Founded in 1884, the combination of 13 breed clubs from America and Canada formed the American Kennel Club. Their mission continues to be advance the education, background and preservation of pure breed dogs.

Blowing the Coat

The term "Blowing the coat" refers to a dog that sheds their coat all at once. Most dogs will do this a couple times a year, shedding a winter coat in the spring for example. While Pugs are fair shedders as it is, a female in heat will shed more than the normal amount or "blow her coat".

Breeder

Person involved in breeding dogs. Most often an enthusiast for a particular breed, the serious breeder pays special attention to preserve the breed and retain the integrity of genetics.

C-Section

Cesarean Section or C-Section is the surgical procedure of giving birth. This is done by making an opening in the abdomen to remove the babies when a vaginal birth is not possible.

Canine Good Citizen

The Canine Good Citizen (CGC) is a two-part program offered through the American Kennel Club promoting responsible pet ownership and canine etiquette.

Certified Trainer

A certified canine trainer will have gone through schooling and a mentorship program to earn a certification in dog training. A dog trainer should continue their education throughout their career by taking knowledge assessments and/or becoming behavior consultant certified.

EKG

Electrocardiogram is a test that is performed to check the electrical activity of the heart. Dogs are hooked up with electrodes to monitor the hearts rhythm to determine whether the heart is working properly.

Heat Cycle

A 28 day cycle when a female pug is ovulating and able to conceive.

Hip Dysplasia

An irregular development of the hip joint. It is genetic, often exacerbated by a Pug's environment. Painfully crippling, hip dysplasia may be treated through medication and/or surgery.

Hot Spot

Also known as acute moist dermatitis, hot spots are red, moist lesions that develop on a dog's head or torso. They tend to grow quickly due to the dog licking or biting at the infected area

Imprint Phase

The imprint phase happens twice in a puppy's life. It is when they are most susceptible to change and perception of new things in their lives. During this time it is important to keep things upbeat and positive or it most likely will have life long, negative effect on a dog's psyche.

Kennel Club

The oldest Kennel Club in the world, the UK Kennel Club was founded by Queen Victoria because of her affection for the Pug. The mission of the KC is to promote, educate and maintain the breed standards of pure breed dogs.

Nasodigital Hyperkeratosis

This condition may occur in dogs and cats, usually on their paws. Occasionally on the nose. Pugs suffer from the nasal version of Hyperkeratosis.

Positive Reinforcement Training

This is the type of training where parents teach good behavior through positive praise. It is often effective in building self-confidence in the canine. Positive reinforcement training is used with a combination of treating and praise.

Puglish
Pug translation from English, however, the wires tend to get crossed between the two.
English "Leave it"
Puglish translation "Must be something to lick and lick and lick"

Puppy Mill

Businesses in the market for making money off of dog breeding. Most of these operations keep their dogs in cages for the duration of their life. As long as the owners provide adequate food, water and shelter they are within the limits of the law.

"Sitting On" Training

A training lesson where the dog is leashed and attached to the owner. The owner must take the dog out to potty every 60 to 90 minutes. It limits the free roam of the dog and puts the parent back in charge. An effective training method for those stubborn dogs that refuse to potty outside.

Temperament

A fancy word for personality. A potential owner may get an idea of the pups personality by interacting with the parents, but then again all dogs are unique.

Whelping Box

Whelping is a fancy term for giving birth. A whelping box is merely a place to have the babies. Often it is a box with high sides so the babies don't wander out of it before they're ready to explore.